Daisy the Dachshund Gets Adopted

By
Shannon King

© 2018 Shannon King
All Rights Reserved.

No part of this book may be reproduced, stored in a retrieval system, or transmitted by any means without the written permission of the author.

First Published by Daisy Mae Books 10/15/2018

ISBN: 978-0-692-04361-5

DAISY MAE BOOKS
Bloomington, Indiana
www.daisymaebooks.com

Hey there! I am Daisy the Dachshund and I am two months old.

Today is a very special day; I'm going to be adopted by my new best friend, Savannah, and her family.

I will miss my family, but Savannah's aunt adopted my sister, Sophie, yesterday so I will have a sister close.

I am so excited to go to my new home!
Savannah and her family are here to pick me up now.

I have never been in a car before.
I have never been anywhere before.

I am a little nervous and I got sick in the car.

My new family is very understanding but I am still sorry I made a mess.

Finally we made it to my new home!

My new family has already bought me food, a bed, a leash, a collar and some new toys.

Savannah took me outside to show me where to go potty. I will try my best not to go potty inside but I am only a puppy and accidents do happen.

My new family understands.

The next thing my family teaches me is my new address and phone number.

It is important to know all these things in case I ever get separated from my family.

Savannah also puts a tag on my collar that has my name, address and phone number on it in case I ever need it.

Savannah's mommy helps her feed me because its very important not to over-feed puppies.

They also give me a bath once a week, clean my teeth, and trim my toenails.

I really love taking a bath, the water is so warm.

Savannah's mommy takes special care not to trim my toenails too short because that can hurt.

Together, my new family and I learn the rules and routines of my new home.

I am their first puppy and we are all learning together.

They will let me know when I am doing something I shouldn't be doing by telling me, "No."

There is a lot to remember but I am doing my best. As long as I am trying my best, my new family is pleased.

There are so many new toys around that sometimes I forget which toys are mine and which ones are Savannah's.

Savannah reminds me by taking her toys away, telling me, "No." and giving me one of my toys to play with.

It is also important to not beg for food or play too rough with other people or dogs.

I am supposed to wait for people to invite me into their laps before I jump on them.

That is a hard manner to remember because I am a very friendly dog and I love people.

Savannah teaches me that when I am told to do something that I must do it immediately.

This is one of the most important rules because my family is trying to keep me safe.

When we go places it is important that I stay near my family. If I don't, I could get into trouble.

Savannah teaches me to stay close to her by telling me to "heel." That means I am supposed to stay close to her heel of her foot.

She also teaches me to sit, stay, shake hands, lay down and roll over.

I am excited to do these tricks because I get treats for doing my best.

Last week we went to the park. I managed to get away from my family to chase a squirrel. My family started yelling my name and telling me to come back.

But I wasn't listening very well and ran into a busy street and I almost got ran over by a truck!

I was so scared that I had an accident in the street and I started crying!

My new family was very relieved that I was okay. I got scolded for not listening to them when they were yelling for me.

I understand now that I have to listen and do as I'm told.

My new family forgave me and now when my family tells me to do something, I do it the first time, every time.

www.ingramcontent.com/pod-product-compliance
Lightning Source LLC
Chambersburg PA
CBHW042145290426
44110CB00002B/116